VEDIC EDUCATION

FROM DARKNESS TO LIGHT

RAMANANDA CAITANYA CANDRA DAS

Copyright © Ramananda Caitanya Candra Das
All Rights Reserved.

ISBN 979-888530134-3

This book has been published with all efforts taken to make the material error-free after the consent of the author. However, the author and the publisher do not assume and hereby disclaim any liability to any party for any loss, damage, or disruption caused by errors or omissions, whether such errors or omissions result from negligence, accident, or any other cause.

While every effort has been made to avoid any mistake or omission, this publication is being sold on the condition and understanding that neither the author nor the publishers or printers would be liable in any manner to any person by reason of any mistake or omission in this publication or for any action taken or omitted to be taken or advice rendered or accepted on the basis of this work. For any defect in printing or binding the publishers will be liable only to replace the defective copy by another copy of this work then available.

His Divine Grace A.C.Bhakthivedanta Swami Prabhupada

Contents

1. Introduction To Bhagavad Gita — 1

2. Guruparampara — 7

3. The Incarnation Of Lord Buddha — 10

4. By Krishna's Mercy, We Can Overcome The Ocean Of Illusion — 17

5. Seeing Krishna In Everything — 21

6. Mantra Meditation — 27

7. Future Predictions — 34

8. Nivar Cyclone — 35

9. Live Life Anxiety Free — 38

Author Intro — 45

CHAPTER ONE

Introduction to Bhagavad gita

Bhagavad Gita

Hare Krishna, I welcome you all for today's evening program we will have Small Harinama sankirtan and study of Bhagavad Gita, Bhagavad Gita contains 18 chapters & 700 slokas Bhagavad Gita is part of Mahabharata which contains 1 lakh verses

16.02 Mahabharata is compiled by Veda Vyasa – written by Vinayaka Today 1st zoom meeting we have there may be some technical faults please excuse us for any mistakes Bhagavad Gita we have to learn through guru parampara Lord Krishna says in the 4th chapter of Bhagavad Gita Evam parampara pramptam imam rajarsayo viduh sakalena yogo nastah paramtapa

17.00 so Bhagavad Gita we have to learn through guru parampara lord Krishna has instructed the Bhagavad Gita to sun god vivasvan he instructed it to ikshvaku Manu in this way it is coming through the guru parampara so we have to learn through this guru parampara any knowledge we get it should be authorized unauthorized many people are giving commentary of Bhagavad Gita they are pushing on their own agenda, their own philosophy, their own concoction

17.43 We have to use Krishna's knowledge, Krishna's Instructions, Krishna's teachings, in his service and not for propagating our own agenda, our own philosophy, or our own concoction, so Bhagavad Gita should not be used like that, Lord Krishna is the Adi guru from him all the knowledge comes so lord Krishna is instructing this Bhagavad Gita to arjuna so arjuna was submissive, arjuna has enquired from Krishna in a submissive mood he was a friend, he was a devotee, so he was a surrendered soul to Krishna, so in this way, Bhagavad Gita was being taught to arjuna so in this way we have to understand through guru paramapara, so there are various parampara, we all know, there is a parampara coming from Lord Brahma, from

Mahalakshmi, Sri Vaishnavas, Sri sampradaya, there is sampradaya from, lord shiva - Rudra sampradaya, vishnuswami from 4 kumara

19.00 we have 4 authorized disciplic succession from mother Lakshmi, Brahma, Shiva, 4 Kumara, so we have to learn Bhagavad Gita through guru paramapara, so this knowledge during the course of time it gets lost, in this way teachings of Bhagavad Gita also said to be lost again Krishna revives it through arjuna so in Bhagavad Gita we can learn 5 things what are those 1. Science of God 2.Nature of living entity, 3. Prakriti, 4. Kala, 5. Karma

We can have five kinds of relationships with lord Krishna what are those 1. One can be in a passive state 2. One can be Servant, like Brother/Sisters 3. Friend, 4. Parents, 5. Lover Husband/Wife

21.00 These are all different kinds of relationship we have, same kinds of relationship exists in the spiritual world in reality whereas in this world it is temporary, one can become lord Krishna's servant, friend, parents, a lover like gopis, Rukmini, Satyabhama and so many wife's of Lord Krishna, another relationship is parents like Vasudev, Devaki, yashodamayi, Kunti Maharani, Nanda maharaja, Vasudev, akrura uncle, uddhava, arjuna, friend, sudhama, and so many gopala friends, we can

22.00

have friendship with Lord Krishna, we can have Lord Krishna as our son or one can have a relationship as a lover or husband, and passive like not close relationship, like plants, trees, animals, they serve in their own capacity, office colleagues, acquaintance, Bhagavad Gita contains 5 topics

1. Science of God, 2. The constitutional position of the living entity, 3. Jiva 4. Ishvara, 5. Prakriti, Karma Lord Krishna is the master we are all his servants.

23.18 Lord Krishna's nature is sat chit ananda, lord Krishna is unlimited we are limited, so these are the differences between lord Krishna & us, lord Krishna is sat chit ananda vigraha he is unlimited and we are limited, Lord Krishna is the controller we are controlled, Lord Krishna is the enjoyer, we are all enjoyed, lord Krishna Is the Purusha we are Prakriti, we are all controlled by lord Krishna, material nature, karma, we are all doing different kinds of activities that are also discussed in Bhagavad Gita.

24.14 lord Krishna is the supreme controller we are controlled, he is the greatest of all living entities, so these are the topics discussed in Bhagavad Gita.

25.00 We must have a deep study of Bhagavad Gita, I am just giving a summary, and we all have 4 kinds of defects.

1. We are sure to commit mistakes 2. We are subject to Illusion or Maya 3. We have a tendency to cheat others 4. We have imperfect senses Every conditioned soul has these 4 defects.

26.00 So Bhagavad Gita is not imparted by a living entity who has these 4 kinds of defects, lord Krishna and acharyas are beyond all kinds defects, we have so many defects, as said above, we think something wrong as right, we don't know what is what, we have imperfect senses, we cheat others also, these are the imperfections every conditioned soul has, Bhagavad Gita is not taught by a conditioned soul, Bhagavad Gita is taught by the perfect super soul is teaching Bhagavad Gita to us, nowadays so many people are giving commentary on Bhagavad Gita.

27.00 Having so many defects, lord Krishna is the controller of Maya, he never cheats, he never commits mistakes, so I will reading guru parampara list

28.00 Lord Krishna instructed Bhagavad Gita to Lord Brahma, Lord Brahma instructed it to Narada muni, Narada muni instructed to vyasadeva, vyasadeva instructed it to madhvacharya then all the acharyas have instructed to their disciples as below Padmanabha, narahari, Madhava, akshobhya, Jaya tirtha, jnanasindhu, daya Nidhi.

29.00 Vidhya Nidhi, Rajendra, jayadharma, Purushottam, brahmanya tirtha, vysatirtha, Lakshmi pati, madhavendra puri, Ishvara puri, Nithyananda, Advaita, Lord Caitanya, Swarup, Sanatana, Raghunath, jiva, Krishna Dasa kaviraja, narottama, Vishwanath Chakravarti Thakura, Baladeva Vidhya Bhushan, Jagannatha Dasa Babaji, Bhaktivinoda Thakura, goura Kishore Dasa Babaji, Bhaktisiddhanta Sarasvati Thakur, Bhaktivedanta Swami Prabhupada, and then His holiness jayapataka swami we are receiving knowledge from him now, in this way in the future this parampara will continue when we will be instructing it to our followers.

Bhagavad Gita 1st chapter is all about observing the armies on the battlefield of Kurukshetra

30.00 Bhagavad Gita was spoken at battlefield, at a scared place, Kurukshetra, when fighting was about to start, any religious activity done their benefits the performer, every place we see there is a place for gambling, there is a place for intoxication, there is a place for illicit sex, there is a place for meat-eating, there is a place for performing religious activities, sacrifices, Kurukshetra is a place suitable for performing religious sacrifices, activities, anything done their It favors the person who performs it

31.00 Pious people and pious activities are rewarded there, impious people go to sinful places, whereas pious people go to holy places like Ganga, Yamuna, Sarasvati, Kaveri, Narmada, Sindhu, So many holy places, rivers are there, pious people go to places where saintly persons live, places of worship of demigods or Lord Vishnu is performed, so lord Krishna is instructing Bhagavad Gita In these holy places, arjuna is receiving knowledge, victory is on lord Krishna side, because Lord Krishna is dharma personified, he establishes dharma

32.00 And vanquishes demons who perform adharma "paritranaya sadhunam vinashayacha duskritam dharma samstapanarthaya sambhavami yuge yuge" B.G.4.9

Lord Krishna appears in every yuga to establish Dharma and vanquish the demons, so here also lord has come to establish Dharma and vanquish demons who are overburdening the earth planets, in kali yuga population of demons have increased, even it has happened during dwapara yuga, Lord Krishna came to reduce the burden of the mother earth planet, so many demons have increased in kali yuga, even it has happened during dwapara yuga, Lord Krishna is clearing the demoniac mentality by asking them to chant his holy name by this method lord Krishna is making them devotees

33.00 Dhritarashtra and Pandu are brothers but Dhritarashtra on account of his blindness from the beggining of his birth, he was not able to occupy the throne, he cannot become king, because of his bodily defects but his younger brother pandu he becomes king, he is healthy, he was energetic, he has conquered the whole earthly planet and he was very chivalrous, he had a lot of power but Pandu dies untimely because of a curse, pandu kills a muni who was engaged in procreation, the muni before dying curses pandu to die in a similar situation. Madri enters the funeral pyre of her husband whereas Kunti maharani remains

34.00

Alive to take care of the 5 remaining children that are Pandavas, here the property dispute has arisen between Dhritarashtra and Pandava this was a dispute to rule over the kingdom, everyone has the right to do their own occupational duty, Brahmanas are supposed to be educating, studying, reading, supposed to be engaged in performing sacrifices, and Kshatriyas are supposed to be ruling, collecting taxes, engaged in performing sacrifices, giving charity whereas vaishyas are supposed to be doing cow protection, farming, trade these are all the activities of vaishyas, whereas sudras are

35.00 Are supposed to be serving other 3 varnas, so arjuna is a Kshatriya, he was asking just 5 villages but they were not ready to give even such a small piece of land, somehow by cheating, by gambling, Dhritarashtra's party Kauravas have gained property of Yudhishthira by cunning methods, by gambling they have acquired/usurped the property of Yudhishthira, they have become kings, but arjuna, Pandavas have the right to rule because they are Kshatriyas they are not supposed to become like a mendicant, they cannot become brahmana, they cannot become vaishyas or Sudras, they have the right to rule,

36.00 They are deprived of their property, so there are 6 kinds of aggressors

1. One who occupies your property
2. One who kidnaps one's wife
3. One who gives poison,
4. One who sets fire to the house
5. One who attacks with deadly weapons,
6. One who plunders the wealth, So these are all aggressors,

Dhritarashtra's son Duryodhana has committed various aggressive activities against Pandavas, they gave poison to Bhima, they set fire to the house in which Pandavas were living and they attacked with deadly weapons, they have tried to disrobe or dishonor Draupadi, keechaka also kidnapped Draupadi, Bhima had killed kichaka.

37.00 So they committed all types of aggressive actions against the Pandavas these types of sinful people can be killed, six types of aggressors can be killed even though they may be blood relatives.

38.00 they have arrived at Kurukshetra to settle their property dispute, they unable to solve the dispute by negotiation, lord Krishna became their messenger they did not accept messages of Lord Krishna, Lord Krishna has requested the Kauravas to give five villages, they have denied even such a small request. So the war is declared now, since Duryodhana was unwilling to spare the land, they were ready for the fight, they do not want to share their kingdom either Kauravas or Pandavas must rule the world.

39.00 they all have assembled here to fight & Settle the dispute Dhritarashtra is asking Sanjaya what is the status he is asking his secretary Sanjaya, Sanjaya is a disciple of Vyasa through him he got special knowledge/empowerment to see things far away. So he is sitting in the palace of Dhritarashtra he is reporting the activities of Kurukshetra what is happening on the battlefield of Kurukshetra Sanjaya is reporting to

Dhritarashtra

40.00 So Duryodhana observes his teacher dronacharya, dronacharya was guru/teacher for both Kauravas and Pandavas So dronacharya goes to his guru and talks to him commander in chief of Dhritarashtra's army, whereas the army of Pandavas was arranged by dhritadyumna.

41.00 Son of dhrupad, Draupadi and dristadyumna they are brother/sisters they are children of dhrupad maharaja, dhrupad Maharaj performs sacrifices, from the sacrificial fire dhritadyumna and Draupadi has appeared, so he goes to dronacharya and introduces the various fighters in both the parties, he appreciates the arrangements of dhridtadyumna and introduces his own soldiers, he introduces soldiers who are ready to fight for him dhristaketu, kasiraja, kurujit, kuntibhoja, saibya.

42.00 There are also yuyudhana, Virata, dhrupad, they are all waiting to fight against arjuna here drupada comes to the side of Duryodhana it is a very interesting point because arjuna was his son in law now he is going to fight against his own son in law. so we will stop here Srila Prabhupada ki jay, grantharaj Srimad Bhagavatam ki jay, we will continue in the next session please chant hare Krishna maha-mantra, so if you want to join our Bhagavad Gita course please contact us at 09611243737, if you want to donate for us you can contact us, or you can donate through our bank account which we will provide unto you, Thank you, Hare Krishna

Hare Krishna Hare Krishna Krishna Krishna Hare Hare

Hare Rama Hare Rama Rama Rama Hare Hare

CHAPTER TWO

Guruparampara

GURU PARAMPARA

Today the topic is Guru Parampara So, we have to learn vedic literatures like bhagavad gita, Srimad Bhgavatham through the guru Parampara. Any knowledge we get, it should be authorized unauthorizedly there are many people who give commentary on Bhagavad Gita. They give their own speculation their own agenda, their own philosophy, they propagate through the Bhagavad Gita, they use Krishna's knowledge Krishna's instructions, Krishna's teachings to propagate their agenda, their philosophy, their concoctions, Bhagavad Gita should not be used like that. Lord Krishna is the Adiguru from him all the knowledge comes. So Lord Krishna is instructing this Bhagavad gita to Arjuna. So Arjuna was very submissive. Arjuna has inquired from Krishna in a submissive mood, and he was a friend, he was a devotee. he was a soul surrendered to Krishna.

1.00

So in this way, Bhagavad Gita was being taught to Arjuna. So, in this way, we have to understand Bhagavad Gita through guru Parampara. So there are various Parampara, we all know. So there is a Parampara coming from lord Brahma, Brahma Parampara. And there is a Parampara coming from Mahalakshmi Sri Vaishnavas, Sri Sampradaya, there is a Sampradaya from Brahma that is called Brahma Sampradaya, there is Sampradaya from Mahalakshmi that is called Sri Sampradaya. There is a Sampradaya from lord Shiva that is Vishnuswamy, There is a sampradaya from Kumara sampradaya. So, we have to gain knowledge through four sampradayas, from Lord Brahma, from Mahalakshmi, from Lord Shiva, from four kumaras, Sanaka Kumara, Sanatana, Sanandana, Sanata kumaras. So this Bhagavad Gita we have to learn through the Guru Parampara. So, any knowledge during the course of time, it gets lost. So in this way Bhagavad Gita also said to be lost again, but Krishna is again establishing the Parampara through

Arjuna. So in Bhagavad Gita, we can learn five things, what are the five things we can learn from Bhagavad Gita we can learn about the science of God, nature of the living entities, and.

THE DISCIPLIC SUCCESSION

Guru Parampara

Evam parampara-praptam imam rajarsayo viduh (Bhagavad-gita, 4.2).

This Bhagavad-gita As It Is is received through this disciplic succession:

1) Krsna
   2) Brahma
   3) Narada
   4) Vyasa
   5) Madhva
   6) Padmanabha
   7) Nrhari
   8) Madhava
   9) Aksobhya
   10) Jaya Tirtha
   11) Jnanasindhu
   12) Dayanidhi
   13) Vidyanidhi
   14) Rajendra
   15) Jayadharma
   16) Purusottama
   17) Brahmanya Tirtha
   18) Vyasa Tirtha
   19) Laksmipati
   20) Madhavendra Puri
   21) Isvara Puri, (Nityananda, Advaita)
   22) Lord Caitanya
   23) Rupa, (Svarupa, Sanatana)
   24) Raghunatha, Jiva
   25) Krsnadasa
   26) Narottama
   27) Visvanatha
   28) (Baladeva) Jagannatha
   29) Bhaktivinoda

30) Gaurakisora
31) Bhaktisiddhanta Sarasvati
32) His Divine Grace A. C. Bhaktivedanta Swami Prabhupada
Source : Bhagavad Gita As It Is - Introduction

• 9 •

CHAPTER THREE

The incarnation of Lord Buddha

The incarnation of Lord Buddha S.B.2.7.37

Even though they know Vedic knowledge but still they are considered as atheists they might have learned from sukracharya Asura guru Is sukracharya, just like balimaharaja story is there it is said that sukracharya knew that lord Vishnu has come previously sukracharya preached to Bali maharaja that Lord Vishnu is supreme we have to offer everything to him now when Vishnu himself has come as Vamana avatar begging, sukracharya could able to understand that he is Lord Vishnu he will take away everything, so he wanted to stop Bali Maharaj from offering everything to lord vamanadeva. Demons or asuras know religious principle but still, they do not follow it, they misrepresent, they utilize them in the wrong way, this is atheism. Who are atheists we can categories, communists are there a joins also considered to be atheist Because they do not follow actual religious principles they follow sub religious principles like non-violence it is commonsense that we should not harm others actual religious principles are given by supreme personality of godhead dharmam tu sakshad bhagavat pranitam. Actual religion is given by god. If God says you kill your father, your guru, your relatives, friends, then we have to follow it that is actual religion so lord Krishna said you kill Bhishma, dronacharya, kill all your relatives, who are against dharma or Krishna, dharmam tu sakshad bhagavat pranitam, whatever God says that is religion

21.00

After atheists becomes more powerful they harm others they are annihilate the inhabitants of different planets, Russian, china inventing many nuclear weapons, now so-called advanced scientists Are always trying to create something which is going to harm others jagato ahita. It is not favorable that is what the scientists are doing by inventing various kinds of advanced weapons, nuclear bombs and go on creating all kinds of disastrous things here the atheist are annihilating the inhabitants of different planets flying unseen in the sky on well-built rockets built by great scientist Maya he is considered to be a great scientist he is an asura he is an architect similar to Vishwakarma but Vishwakarma is a demigod whereas Maya is an asura.

They all are experts in various material science for Pandavas he has built Indraprastha city capital city of Pandavas and also a palace in that city because of this palace Duryodhana got bewildered thinking water to be land and land to be water he got confused and fell down due to which

23.00 Draupadi laughed, that palace is built by Maya asura, so asuras are experts in architectural science Lord in order to bewilder atheist he will also become atheist Buddha. If you want to preach to someone you also have to adapt the principles of them in that way you can preach to them it is said birds of the same feather flock together so the same group of people work together. Similarly, in order to preach to the atheist's lord Buddha dressed like an atheist, he preached sub religious principles like nonviolence

24.00 it is said that the Buddha incarnation mentioned in this verse is not of this present age. According to Srila jiva Gosvami the Buddha incarnation appeared in different kali yuga. So in the duration of the life of one Manu, there are more than 72 kali yugas and in one of them Buddha appears, during that time people were misutilizing the Vedic principle. There is mention of animal sacrifice in Vedas but since there are no qualified Brahmanas it is said that there are five things that are forbidden in kali yuga

1. Asvamedham – horse sacrifice,
2. Gavalambham-Cow sacrifice
3. Sanyasam-Renounced order of life
4. Pala paitrikam- offering of flesh to the forefather
5. Devarenasutautpattim-Begetting children from husbands younger brother

Kalau Pancha vivarjayet - so these five things are forbidden in kali yuga in that way these people were misutilizing Vedic principles and they were killing animals in the name of Vedic sacrifices. In order to stop

26.00 this violence against animals lord Buddha as compassionate father of all living entities appeared and preached non-violence as the highest form of religion he is one among the 10 incarnations of Lord Vishnu/

Krishna Lord Buddha appeared at a time when people are most materialistic and preaches common-sense religious principles like ahimsa. Such ahimsa is not a religious principle actually when there is a war there cannot be nonviolence. Even in politics also nonviolence will not workout sometimes you may have to use force

27.00 Sometimes violence may require in order to conquer rebellious kingdoms if there is a religious war there is no question of nonviolence. There are various aggressors who attack with deadly weapons, kidnap one's wife, we have to act violently and kill the miscreants what kind of nonviolence we can preach to the miscreants there are 4 methods of ruling

1. Sama –pacifying or music

2. Dhana – by giving away in Charity

3. Bheda – Division divide and rule people from the UK Have divided us and ruled us

4. Danda – Punishment

6 types of aggressors mentioned above must be punished.

Murderers are supposed to be hanged, danda niti. So one living entity is the food for another living entity in that way violence is sometimes required All flesh-eating animals like lions and tigers have to be violent in order to have their food you cannot preach nonviolence to them. How can you expect peacefulness in flesh-eating animals Prabhupada mentions that India got independence from foreign rulers like Britishers due to Netaji Subhash Chandra Bose. Gandhi preached nonviolence for many years he was not highly successful But Netaji Subhash Chandra Bose organizes the Indian national army he went abroad and tie-up with Germany, Japan in that way he expanded the strength of Indians this the Britishers felt uneasy to handle because they were ruling India with the support of Indians now Indians are acting against them so they felt uneasy to handle Indians so naturally they have to quit India. So India got independence because of ahimsa that is commonly said but there is himsa also. Nobody likes to have violence in their kingdom. Britishers had experienced a lot of violence in India so that's why they left India.

31.00 So being nonviolent is not actually a religious principle but it is also an important quality for persons who are actually religious. We should not unnecessarily harm others. If there is any Religious cause then one can become violent just like the battle of Kurukshetra. We can take an example an army man at the time of war kills he is awarded for his bravery when the same person comes and kills innocent persons in the civil society he is punished similarly if it is for religious cause one can become violent for a murderer, thief or rioter how are you going control him you may have to be violent in that way you can control the attackers

33.00 Recently also after the Jallikattu protest suddenly violence has increased in order to disperse the crowd the police have to use their power. It is said that a lot of traitors have also joined them. Actual people who were fighting for jallikattu have left But traitors do not want to close down the protest; they still want to continue the protest So in order to chase them away police have to use force, so violence is required sometimes.

34.00 a dog is coming to bite you at That moment you cannot be peaceful or nonviolent you may have necessary steps to defend yourself since a mad street dog will not understand your peace message so you have to use your strength to defend against the cruel animals. You take a stone or stick it will be afraid, Similarly monkey also I have seen a lot of monkeys on pilgrimage tours, the monkey may want to bite you or want to take away your eyeglasses, purse or Japa mala, my Japa mala one monkey has taken in sholinghur big/Small hill it tore away Japa mala and bite the beads Animals cannot understand our peace message if we just keep a stick in our hand animals may not try to harm us, Similarly, Cows or bulls just to frighten them Cowherd boys keep sticks

35.00 Similarly children also, so violence is required sometimes, one living entity is food for another living entity. Joins are preaching nonviolence jiva himsa Ours is different we take Krishna prasadam so there is no question violence or nonviolence but joins are not like that they only take vegetarian foods, even in vegetarian foods life exists so many seeds, grains plants, life exists

36.00 Nonvegetarians kill one animal and eat vegetarians take grains they take many many living entities. We Krishna devotees take Krishna prasadam neither vegetarian nor Non-Vegetarian. So any activity we do we should do it as a sacrifice to Lord Vishnu, Because all our activity generate some reaction it may be good or bad when it is done as a sacrifice to Lord Vishnu there is no question of good or bad everything will be good Bhoktaram yajna tapasam Sarva Loka maheshwaram

Work done as a sacrifice for Lord Vishnu has to be performed otherwise work causes bondage in this material world. You Receive or give away in charity, perform sacrifice or austerity all has to be done for lord Vishnu. Then we do not get any reaction, but if we do it for ourselves then there is a reaction we get entangled in the cycle of repeated birth and death.

But before learning these principles of nonviolence one has to learn other two principles namely to be humble and to be prideless. Unless one is humble and prideless one cannot be harmless and nonviolent. Actually, we should think that this world is not ours we have come here temporarily and will be leaving this world at any moment. So in that way, we should be humble whatever we have is given to me by the supreme personality of godhead we should engage it back in his service. We should be humble and not be proud.

38.00 many kings in the past have thought themselves to be proprietors of their kingdoms that's why they have lost their kingdoms, if they would have thought that this kingdom is Lord Krishna's and I am his servant it should be engaged in his service alone and not for one's personal sense enjoyments. They were proud of their royal status and have failed to engage themselves in the service of the lord because of which they have become proud and autocratic and were not following guru sadhu and sastra. Mleccha, Yavana kings who have ruled India have thought that we are rulers whatever we say you have to follow. It is said that on the one hand they had their Scripture and in another hand they had a sword and they have threatened that either you accept our religion or you become killed by our Sword. In this way, they misutilized their power and have expanded their kingdom. They were not humble, they were proud of their religion. Unless one is humble and prideless one cannot be harmless and nonviolent and after being nonviolent one has to learn tolerance, simplicity of living we should be tolerant, sometime minor offenses may be committed unknowingly by others

40.00 We should lead a simple life simple living and high thinking instead of that we are complicating our life more and more. Now we are entirely dependent on others for our fuel Supply that is Crude oil. We have created an artificial lifestyle, In the past, we had animals as our mode of conveyance, there were some horses used to travel 1000s of kilometers, and bullock carts due to which there were no accidents or fuel crisis, food crisis. etc now they have created motor cars for this they need petrol/Diesel for this some workers has to work under the ocean. If there is a shortage of petrol then everything will be collapsed prices of food grains will increase and many riots/Strikes may occur.

41.00 We have created an artificial lifestyle we should learn to lead a simple life whatever is naturally available we should utilize it and be satisfied with it. Instead of utilizing horses and bulls for transportation or agricultural purposes, they are eating their flesh. There will be no petrol problem if we engage bulls/Horses for our conveyances. No accidents no injuries no deaths, no need for insurances, etc. We use fruits/Vegetables and through away skin, the animals will eat it. God is maintaining every living entity we should make our life as simple as possible. One must offer respect to great religious preachers/ Leaders

42.00 Because it is said that guru as good as hari, sakshad haritvena samasta sastrair yuktas thata bhavyatha yeva sadbhih So guru is as good as god We cannot control our senses if we are not engaged in the service of Lord Krishna, hrishikena hrishikesa sevanam we should engage all our senses in the service of master of senses. Then our senses will be in our control we should not be too much attached to family, etc we should give them basic necessities, but we should not be too much attached to them, the ultimate goal of all religious principle is to become a devotee of Lord Krishna. Lover of god, in religious principle there must be a god in the center. So all these Non-Violence

44.00 Honesty, Truthfulness these are all sub religious principles, they are not the main religious principles, generally known as up dharma or nearness to religious principles. So sometimes in politics or even in our own day-to-day activities, we have to take the help of advocates, the profession of advocates is such that they have to lie otherwise they may be finding difficulty in their profession. Even in business sometimes they have to tell a lie otherwise they may be having difficulty in running their business.

45.00 Ksatriyas have to be violent sometimes they may also have to tell lies, also cheat. Same in business also. These things are unavoidable under certain emergency situations. So anything we do we should do it as a sacrifice for Lord Krishna, then we will not be having any reaction to it. If we do it for our own sense gratification then we will suffer or enjoy the results. We may have to take repeated birth and death. Arjuna as a Kshatriya and grihastha has fought for his rights he had killed his own relatives, teachers because all of them have become liberated from their sinful life.

46.00 So anything which is pleasing to Lord Krishna this is actual religion it is said once yudhisthira maharaja was asked by lord Krishna to tell a lie unto droncharya about the death of his son aswathama, he has never lied in his life he was in dilemma as to how to tell a lie unto his own guru dronacharya, he was following sub religious principle of truthfulness, Supreme personality of godhead is telling here to tell a lie but yudhisthira maharaja was reluctant he was not obeying the command of lord Krishna.

It is extremely difficult to defeat dronacharya in the battlefield and he will not die until unless he hears the death news of his own son. Somehow yudhisthira maharaja took the courage to tell a lie he said that "aswathama iti kunjara hatah"

47 He said an elephant called aswathama had died but dronacharya had thought that his own son had died. In this way dronacharya died lamenting the death of his dear son. Sometime in an emergency situation you may have to tell lies. But only if it is sanctioned by lord Krishna.

Grantharaj srimad bhagavatam ki jay

Srila Prabhupada ki jay

Ananta koti Vaishnava vrind ki jay

CHAPTER FOUR

By Krishna's mercy, we can overcome the ocean of illusion

Reading from S.B.2.7.42

yesam sa esa bhagavan dayayed anantah

sarvatmanasrita-pado yadi nirvyalikam

te dustaram atitaranti ca deva-mayam

naisam mamaham iti dhih sva-srgala-bhaksye

Translation and Purport by

His Divine Grace A.C.Bhakthivedanta Swami Prabhupada

TRANSLATION

But anyone who is specifically favored by the Supreme Lord, the Personality of Godhead, due to unalloyed surrender unto the service of the Lord, can overcome the insurmountable ocean of illusion and can understand the Lord. But those who are attached to this body, which is meant to be eaten at the end by dogs and jackals, cannot do so.

PURPORT

The unalloyed devotees of the Lord know the glories of the Lord in the sense that they can understand how great the Lord is and how great is His expansion of diverse energy. Those who are attached to the perishable body can hardly enter into the realm of the science of Godhead. The whole materialistic world, based on the conception of the material body as the self, is ignorant of the science of God. The materialist is always busy working for the welfare of the material body, not only his own but also those of his children, kinsmen, community men, countrymen, etc. The materialists have many branches of philanthropic and altruistic activities from a political, national, and international angle of vision, but none of the fieldwork can go beyond the jurisdiction of the misconception of identifying the material body with the spirit soul. Unless, therefore, one is saved from the wrong conception of the body and the soul, there is no knowledge of Godhead, and unless there is knowledge of God, all advancement of material civilization, however dazzling, should be considered a failure.

Invocation mantra guru pranama mantras,

Hare Krishna Hare Krishna Krishna Krishna Hare Hare

Hare Rama Hare Rama Rama Rama Hare Hare

Lecture by His Grace Ramananda Caitanya Chandra Das

By Krishna's mercy, we can overcome the ocean of illusion

14.00 Krishna is just like the sun, and Maya is just like darkness wherever there is Krishna there is no Maya, similarly wherever there is sun there is no darkness, the devotees who are engaged in constant unalloyed, unmotivated, devotional service to Lord Krishna they can overcome the insurmountable ocean of illusion and understand the lord otherwise it is not possible to understand Krishna, it is impossible to conquer Maya, Krishna says in Bhagavad Gita that "mama Maya duratyaya' his illusory energy is very difficult to overcome, but those who have surrendered to him only can overcome his illusory energy or Maya.

15.00 And it is also said that without the empowerment of Krishna one cannot preach the holy name of Lord Krishna, so those who are spreading the holy name of Lord Krishna are not ordinary souls, they are empowered by Lord Krishna, so we should not blaspheme them, that is one of the offenses against chanting the holy name and on another occasion lord Brahma was in his incarnation as Haridas Thakur there was an attempt to ruin his character by a prostitute, a zamindar had employed a prostitute to ruin or spoil the character of Haridas Thakur.

16.00 Haridas Thakur accepted the proposal of a prostitute since he had taken a vow to chant the holy name of Lord Krishna until he completes that he cannot fulfill the desire of the prostitute so he had asked her to sit and listen to his chanting the holy name and wait until he finishes his chanting, the prostitute also waits one day, two days, on the third day she becomes purified of her sinful desires and expresses her evil intentions, Haridas Thakur knowing her sinful intentions has allowed her to hear his chanting of holy name just for her purification later on she becomes his disciple, she becomes a devotee, so only devotees like Haridas Thakur can overcome the insurmountable ocean of illusion and understand the lord. Only devotees can overcome the desire for sexual life others cannot overcome it, It is impossible.

17.00 only devotees can understand Krishna through their devotional service, "sevonmukhe hi jihvadau svayam Eva sphurat adah" only by service we can understand, only devotees can overcome illusory energy of lord other's cannot overcome it and those who are attached to the body which is going to be eaten at the end by jackals, dogs cannot do so, so those who are attached to this body, which is ultimately going to be destroyed either by burning in the fire and becoming ash or being thrown over the mountain to vultures, dogs, birds, jackals, non-devotees cannot understand the insurmountable energy of Krishna.

18.40 So those who think that this body made up of earth, water, ether, air, fire, mind, intelligence, as one's own self they are no better than cow's and asses, sa evah go kharah

19.00 so how can cow's and asses understand the supreme personality of godhead,

20.00 we see the materialist are engaged in working hard accumulating money not only for himself but also for his children, his relatives, his community, his country, this is called extended selfishness, now when I get money, I want my family members. Relatives to enjoy and then we want our community men, our caste men, our countrymen also enjoy this is extended selfishness, now we are seeing so many charitable institutions working for the welfare of the material body, forgetting the actual existence of the soul, without caring for the soul.

21.00 They only want to benefit the material body, which is ultimately going to be eaten by jackals, vultures, dogs, ash, the stool of worms, birds, now we are seeing many philanthropic, altruistic activities and many people want to eradicate poverty, hunger, untouchability, they want to get equal rights to all human being, women, animal welfare, etc so many welfare activities are being performed by the materialists they are also opening hospitals, colleges, schools, everything which is done for the body will be destroyed, no ultimate benefit for the spirit soul. So there is no gain doing welfare work for the body alone which is going to be destroyed.

23.20 Until unless one understands that one is not this body and that he is soul, the soul belongs to god it is part and parcel of god, until unless this knowledge is there all the advancement of modern material civilization, however dazzling should be considered a failure. "Srama eva hi kevalam" hard labor for nothing. Whatever we do in this world ultimate perfection should be realizing oneself and Narayana "ante narayana smrtih", whatever we do in this world as a brahmana, ksatriya, vaishya, sudra, Brahmachari, grihastha, vanaprastha, sanyasi, whatever may be our occupation ultimately we should remember Narayana at the end of our life, if this is not achieved whatever we do all will be considered a failure, going to different planets or building skyscrapers or building flyovers, or advancement of technology all are considered to be a failure.

25.00 Who are the materialist let's analyze, Mayavadis are the materialists, Maya means this matter Vadis means those who stick to the principle of matter there are different kinds of materialists we should.

26.00 Existence of living entities on the other planets, or many other things like life comes from chemicals, they are all mental speculators, nowadays Astanga yoga is very popular so many yogis, Babaji's are coming out with various schemes, plans, programs to give you spiritual perfection by bodily gymnastic exercises, tone up your body, muscle up your body, reduce fat, become slim, beautiful, cure for diseases, there are so many so-called yogis are there.

27.50 We see big companies having big businesses share market, so many big business magnets are there working day and night simply for sense gratification that's all they are called karmis

28.00 jnanis means finding out solutions by mental speculations and yogis means they are finding out solutions by spiritual salvations by bodily exercises they are all in strict sense materialist there is no question of spiritualism

28.20

C.C.ADILILA 7.39-43, San franscisco 1.2.1967

CHAPTER FIVE

Seeing Krishna in Everything

SEEING KRISHNA IN EVERYTHING
Speaker : By Ramananda Caitanya Candra Das
SRI GOPALBHATTA GOSVAMI EDUCATIONAL CENTRE

1.00

So today the topic is seeing god Krishna in everything/everywhere there are 9 planets Each planet represent different incarnations of Lord Krishna/ Lord Vishnu Sun represents Rama incarnation, Moon represents Krishna Incarnation, Mars represents Narasimhadev incarnation, Venus represents Parasurama incarnation, Jupiter represents Vamana incarnation, Mercury represents Buddha Incarnation, Saturn represents Kurma incarnation, Rahu represents Varaha Incarnation, Kethu represents Matsya Incarnation

3.00

From Surya vamsa Rama has incarnated from Chandra vamsa Krishna has incarnated, we all will be attached anyone incarnation some people will be attached to Rama, Krishna, Narasimha, Buddha, Parasurama, Vamanadev, Kurma, Varaha, Matsya, 9 planets, 9 incarnations so we will be attached to some incarnations of Lord Vishnu.

4.00 Each incarnation did different things/Pastimes they gave different instructions for us they performed different lilas, they lead us in a particular way, how to lead this life in a happy way first is Rama was a perfect householder, perfect son, perfect king, perfect husband, he set an example as an ideal Family Man for all of us, & Then Lord Krishna perfect child to Yashodhamayi, Nanda maharaja.

5.00 perfect child to Devaki, Vasudev, perfect lover to Radharani, perfect friend to Arjuna in this way he has enacted his lilas, perfect brother to Subhadra and Balaram, perfect friend to sudhama, all the cowherd's boys, Lord Krishna is complete Bhagavan Krishna acted as a motherly way because he incarnated in Chandra vamsa, Caitanya Mahaprabhu also acted like a mother.

6.00 Sun, Moon, Mars, Narasimhadev, lord Narasimha dev destroys all the demons, and then sammohaya surah dvisah, those who are against lord Vishnu, Buddha incarnation has bewildered the enemies of lord and his devotees, surah dvisah, he acted like an atheist, he rejected Vedas but he is an incarnation of Lord Vishnu and then Parashurama he killed/chopped the head of all the Kshatriyas who acted inimically towards Brahmanical culture.

7.00 He chopped off the head of all Kshatriyas so-called Kshatriyas, those who are against brahminical culture are not considered to be Kshatriyas they may be called as dvija bandhus, they are punished by Parashurama he punished miscreant Kshatriya rulers by killing them 21 times, from the planet Venus comes Parashurama incarnations so he had killed all impious kstariyas without any restriction.

8.00 Lord Vamanadeva has come as a beggar brahmana and begged 3 footsteps of land from Bali Maharaja and he conquered 3 planetary systems he came as a beggar brahmana, small dwarf brahmana begged 3 footsteps of land from Bali Maharaja and he regained 3 planetary systems offered it back to his elder brother lord Indra, vamanadeva is called as Upendra so from Jupiter comes Vamana incarnation, kurma incarnation comes from Saturn, it acted like a pivot–platform for churning of Mandara mountain, milk ocean, Mandara mountain was sinking In milk ocean, it has to be supported by some platform so kurma avatar has helped in this situation, lord has incarnated as a tortoise & facilitated the churning of milk ocean pastime, so there are various good qualities In asuras and devas when they both combine together to churn milk ocean many good things has come of course poison has come initially which was swallowed by Lord Shiva greatest Vaishnava later on so many good things has appeared airavata elephant, ucchaisrava horse, so many jewels.

10.00 Apsaras, Mahalakshmi & after that nectar has come most important Part nectar has come, later on, Mohini incarnation has appeared danvantari incarnation has come his Mohini incarnation can be categorized to Venus planet, nowadays people are attached to some or other incarnation of Lord Vishnu.

11.00 And then Varaha incarnation has appeared from Rahu planet Varaha avatar picked earth from garbodhaka ocean, boar incarnation after searching even in impure things some good things will come, so he goes to impure places and searches like that lord have taken the form of Varaha and replace bhumandala in its proper place, Varaha incarnation comes from planet Rahu so then next is Matsya avatar, which saved all of us when there was devastation fish or Matsya incarnation has saved all of us planet earth and its inhabitants.

12.06 so like that this world actually is guided by the network of Matsya avatar This fish incarnation is protecting all of us when there is the devastation that time lord will protect us similarly now devastation is happening all over the world, so this Matsya avatar is protecting us like a boat, Similarly ISKCON is considered to be like a fish incarnation it is protecting all of us when there is devastation.

13.00 So we have nine planets and 9 incarnations, also we have dashavatar stotra by Srila jayadeva Gosvami, we all have to remember the pastimes of Lord Krishna daily, 10 incarnations of the lord are Rama, Krishna, Narasimha, Buddha, Parasurama, Vamana, Kurma, Varaha, Matsya these nine incarnations we have to remember every day, Lord Krishna is the source of all incarnations, Krishna Prema is being freely distributed by Sri Caitanya Mahaprabhu Lila is been given to us such that we always remember these lilas every day.

14.00 Acharyas have revived Vedic culture in the world, Srila Prabhupada had revived Krishna consciousness dormant in all of us otherwise because of association of bad elements, duratmas we also became duratmas, by association with great souls Prabhupada we are all becoming devotees so we all have to associate with mahajanas there are 12 mahajanas, Swayambhu, Narada, Sambhu, Kumara, Kapila, Manu, Janako, Bhisma, Bali, Vaiyasaki, Yamaraj. We have to follow in the footsteps of these 12 mahajanas.

15.00 In kaliyuga ocean of faults is there but there is one great quality that is chanting the holy name of Lord Krishna we can go back to the spiritual world, kali kale Krishna namarupa avatar, lord Krishna has descended in his holy name, there is no other incarnation in kali yuga at the end of kali yuga, Kalki avatar will take place, it is like lord Narasimha/ Parashurama so this will happen at the end of kali yuga.

16.00 Lord Caitanya Mahaprabhu has come as a devotee, he has given us Krishna Prema without considering who is qualified and who is not qualified, namo maha vadanyaya Krishna Prema pradayate krishnaya Krishna Caitanya namne gouratvise Namah Lord Caitanya Mahaprabhu is giving us Krishna Prema most magnanimous, merciful love of godhead, so we all have to take advantage of this mercy of lord, Caitanya Mahaprabhu and practice spiritual life become happy in this life and the next so there are so many people who don't take advantage of this mercy of Lord Krishna.

17.00 Lord Caitanya Mahaprabhu, those who are very cruel, very selfish, acting in an envious way creating enmity, division, people are having all unwanted habits, greedy, angry, lusty, enviousness, jealousy, illusion, madness, All kinds of bad qualities is seated in mind, this mind needs to be cleansed by chanting hare Krishna maha-mantra.

18.00 chant as much as possible then we can be happy in this life, even in this kali yuga in the earthly planet kali kale Krishna Nama rupa avatar, he has incarnated as his holy name, so we all commit various offenses there are 7 mothers, birth mother, brahmana's wife, king's wife, planet earth, cow, nurse.

19.00 Demons are committing various offenses to these mothers by polluting water, digging/excavating for petrol/oil wells polluting the earth with various dangerous chemicals, desertifying the planet earth, polluting water reservoirs causing great distress to mother earth, Ganges, rivers, cows, killing Brahmanas, all mothers are troubled, they perform great sinful activities because of which they suffer, the demons die untimely, getting various types of diseases, poverty-stricken condition, starvation.

21.00 Devoid of knowledge on account of offenses to Brahmanas and their wife, no proper knowledge or culture king's wife, they are serving stranger's enemies, foreign nationals, so the demons have very weak mind demons must be having some kind of affliction to mind or their nature/ race is like that even maybe among demons there are pious people they respect the earth, preserve water, everything we get because of our good or bad deeds offenses to earth we suffer poverty-stricken, financial problems, earth represents money Lakshmi if the earth is not kept in a proper way we suffer.

23.00 Financial problems by polluting water we suffer from watery diseases, shortage of food grains, water do not respect brahmana's wife difficulty in understanding brahminical culture, knowledge, offenses to king's wife, living in the country we may have to vacate the country.

24.00

Ultimately whatever suffering we are undergoing is because of our offenses to mother, father, wife children, brother, animals, so many offenses we commit knowingly or unknowingly, because of these offenses we suffer in our life there is a record of every one of our activities, there are various agents like sun, moon, so many planets are watching us they are all witness to our actions, Indra, Chandra, Varuna, Vayu, asta dikpalakas are there they are all watching and giving the judgment, So whatever offenses we commit we suffer from that. Whatever good things we do we enjoy on account of that.

25.00 so this is very important so these 9 planets represent nine incarnations of the lord so any planet adversely placed from that planet we suffer, so if the sun is adversely placed we suffer from king's, or parents, especially father if moon planet is adversely placed or weak we suffer from mother, motherly ladies, elderly ladies, cows, water, mind any offenses we commit to any of our relations that problems we suffer, sun-father, moon-mother, mars-younger brother, police, army, they are protecting us So any offenses to these kinds of people we suffer from them.

26.00 mercury problems in business dealings, intellectual problems, weak Venus problems with relationships, wife, semen, weak Jupiter, financial problems, we have problems among teachers, spiritual matters, temples, etc. Weak Saturn problems with servants, iron, wood,

27.00 Labourers, etc Weak Rahu problems with Abrahamic religious people, problems with Tantric, Ghostly creatures, Kethu-Tantrics, Ghostly creatures, Abrahamic religions, because of offending father, mother ghostly population has increased by offending parents one becomes a ghost, pisacha, pisacha dharma followers are offenders of parents. If you commit offenses to your sister, wife, female servants we suffer trouble from them a female ghosts, female witches, etc

29.00 Wife will divorce, impotency, kidney-related problems, problems in relationships, not very happy relationships, so weak Jupiter financial problems may arise, problems from temple authorities, monks.

30.00 ultimately nine planets represent 9 incarnations of Lord Vishnu and different relationships also, so any suffering we undergo will come under these nine planets.

31.00 Our entire body is controlled by these 9 planets, every ingredient in our body that is earth, water, ether, air, fire, mind, intelligence, ego, all these eight ingredients are controlled by these 9 planets our ego-by sun planet, lord shiva, king, Indra, ego is strong, father, managing authority, is helping you, demigods are helping you the kings or god's are helping you

32.00 if your moon is strong your mother is helping you, motherly ladies are helping you and Durga, Mahalakshmi is helping you, if your moon is weak womanly ladies will not helping you, problems with women, water, plants, trees, animals like cows, problems with childbirth, in one's own mind, all these things will happen, when there are weak mars there could be a shortage of blood, shortage of energy to work, shortage of courage, problems with police, land, construction workers, drivers, Etc all these things will happen. We will continue in the next session

Thank you, Hare Krishna

CHAPTER SIX

Mantra Meditation

Hare Krishna Welcome to today's session on mantra meditation so let's all together chant the Hare Krishna Maha-mantra so this will give peace in our life we are all having so much anxiety now may be due to this corona pandemic we are suffering from various anxiety let's chant this hare Krishna maha-mantra which will free us all of all these anxiety this material world is full of anxiety, we always suffering three folds miseries through body, mind, though other living entities.

1.00 Through natural calamities adhidaivika, adhiboutika, adhyatmika, we are always troubled by these three kinds of miseries so this material world is considered to be dukhalyam asasvatam, full of miseries and it is temporary, only hope is chanting the name of Lord Krishna in kali yuga 1000s of faults will be there but there is only one great quality that is Chanting the holy name of Lord Krishna this will give us relief from all kinds of miseries at least it will give us peace in our life. Lord Krishna is the master of the entire universe He is the enjoyer of all austerity, sacrifices we do.

02.10 He is the friend of all living entities this is the peace formula, we all are thinking that we are proprietors of all the universe, this pandemic has originated from our neighbor china so they want to dominate the other countries or whole world our neighbor china America is leading the world china spreading this pandemic it is considered to be like a bio war. So we have to understand that.

3.00 lord Krishna Is the creator, God is the generator, operator, destroyer, so when god decides things Are destroyed no individual can destroy anybody, So we are all instruments, It is our own karma that we are suffering or enjoying we cannot blame any third person, of course, we are always troubled by threefold miseries through body, mind, through other living entities, through natural calamities, we are all troubled by threefold miseries. So our enemy is our own mind, when the mind is in our control it is acting like a friend when the mind is not in our control it acts like an enemy.

4.00 So this is very important That we try to control our mind, controlling the mind is very very important to mind is unsteady always wavering it is hankering after something sometimes it is lamenting for something, it is always hankering and lamenting. Now Somebody is leading the world now we want to lead the world, later previously the UK Was leading the world past, now America is leading the world, now china is trying to lead the world, so like that there is a competition between each other countries they want to dominate among the demigods and demons also there is a competition, demigods are the natural they have achieved that position because of pious acts.

5.00 Different people are being allotted different places to live there are eight directions each direction one demigod rules, Eastern direction demigods Lord Indra rules, Southern direction Ancestors rule, western direction asuras rule, northern direction Kubera rules, Southeastern direction Agni or fire god rules, Northeastern direction Lord Shiva, Brihaspati deva guru rules, Northwestern direction Ketu or Vayu or moon rules, the Western direction is ruled by Varuna, the southwestern direction is ruled by nirriti or Rahu, in this way there are 8 directions in each direction different demigods reside.

6.00 So we all have to control the mind that is very important, we all have to chant the holy name of Lord Krishna, let us all chant one round of hare Krishna maha-mantra, Jaya Sri Krishna Caitanya Prabhu Nithyananda Sri Advaita gadhadhara srivasadi goura bhakta Vrinda.

Hare Krishna Hare Krishna Krishna Krishna Hare Hare Hare Rama Hare Rama Rama Rama Hare Hare – Minimum 108 times

17.36.

So thank you very much for all of you for watching my video, I request all of you to chant the hare Krishna maha-mantra daily as much as possible daily 108 into 2,3,4,5 make a commitment daily chant hare Krishna maha-mantra at least 108 times

18.00 You can chant more we are all chanting 108into 16 times that 1728 times of Hare Krishna maha-mantra, complete mantra. You all can chant the Hare Krishna maha-mantra maybe 108 times or 1008 times. As per your convenience, you can chant but make a commitment daily chant Hare Krishna maha-mantra you can chant a fixed number of rounds, maybe 4 rounds or 10 rounds, please chant at least 108 times. If you have more time please chant more number of rounds 2,4,6,8 as per your convenience you can chant in the morning or evening also.

19.00 Better is chanting early morning before sunrise getup takes bath and chant hare Krishna mantra in a very nice atmosphere, is peaceful all are most of the people will be taking rest so in villages they all get up early in the morning and they clean the house and street, they all go out for farming works so get up early before sunrise and chant this hare Krishna mantra, wash face mouth and chant the mantra.

20.00 All the ISKCON Temples we chant early in the morning, we get up early in the morning take bath wear new or fresh clothes, attend man gala arati and then we have Japa session we will continuously chant for two hours 16 rounds of hare Krishna mantra, then we go for darshan arati, first, we have Mangala arati. And then Tulasi arati and we have Japa session then we have Darshana arati, guru puja, then Srimad Bhagavatam class, this is our daily sadhana in ISKCON Temples. So make a habit of chanting Hare Krishna maha-mantra daily early in the morning. Very good time very peaceful atmosphere, no much anxiety, very satvic, sattva guna s predominant, afternoon Rajo guna is predominant, in the night time it is tamo guna, So three Gunas 24 hours is divided into 3 sections first 8 hours is sattva guna next eight hours is rajo guna, next eight hours is tamo guna. The first 8 hours early in the morning before sunrises that is called Brahma muhurta up to 12.00 AM is sattva guna is predominant, next from afternoon 12'o clock to 8 PM it is rajo guna, after 8O clock, it is tamo guna starts, up to Brahma muhurta.

22.00 So like that 24hours 3gunas are there. It is always working time is divided into 3 sections Rajo, sattva, tamo Early morning sattva guna, afternoon rajo guna, night time it is tamo guna, stva guna is favorable for all kinds of devotional services, all kinds of austerities, the charity also, early morning we can give charity, austerity we can do. All these things are very nice to do in the early morning, the performance of sacrifice, austerity, charity, early in the morning is very good, the afternoon is rajasic they go out for earning money, business, sales, in the afternoon, in the evening time is good for resting, we all have to rest in the night time, so tamo guna creation, maintenance, and destruction are always happening in this world, now this pandemic is like a destruction world is getting destroyed, again it will be created, so people have died, me people will take birth again, so the soul is immortal maybe some people will die today because of this pandemic but again they will take birth, all the people who have died due to pandemic they will take birth again as per their consciousness, Lord Krishna says in Bhagavad Gita "yam vapi smaran Bhavan tyajatyante kalevaram", whatever state of mind we are we will take birth again Next if we are thinking about Krishna we will take birth among Krishna consciousness devotee family.

24.00 We may go to krishnloka as per our consciousness we get birth. If you are thinking about some celebrity, film star, you may take birth in such family, if you are thinking about our ancestors we will take birth among ancestors, we will be worshipping some ghosts, spirits, they will take birth among them, if somebody is worshipping ancestors he will take birth among them if somebody is worshipping demigods he will take birth among them, if somebody is worshipping ghosts and spirits, black magic is there they will take birth among them, those who worship Krishna they will take birth among them, so Krishna has different incarnations somebody worshipping Rama incarnations he will take birth in Ayodhya, someone worshipping Krishna incarnation he will take birth in Vrindavan, Mathura, Dwaraka, Caitaya maha Prabhu in navadweep, Mayapur, Jagannath puri also we have different people worship.

25.00 Different incarnations of Lord Krishna, so they all take birth there different planets are there Sun, Moon, Mars, Mercury, Jupiter, Venus, Saturn, Rahu, Kethu So nine planets are there we all take birth in these planets we all are getting benefits from these planets, there is a creative planet, there are planets which are destroying, there are planets which are maintaining sun maintains all the universe through its light, heat because of sun we can see everything. Krishna is like the sun, because of Krishna we can see everything clearly, Krishna Surya Samaha mayahoy andhakar, Maya means darkness, darkness means ignorance, so nighttime it is darkness.

26.00 So night time it is Ignorance, in the day time sun is there, early morning, light is their sunrise so soft radiance, the afternoon is fearsome radiance rays, night time again decreasing the rays, sunrise, midday sun, Evening sun, these things are a phenomenon, we get various facilities through the planets, sun planet we get heat, light through sun planet other planets sustain sun evaporates water and profusely gives rain.

27.00 there is the formation of cloud because of sun, the sun evaporates water and there is a cloud, then there is rain, the sun planet, moon planet nourishes all living entities, we all get various fruits juices through the moon, all the fruits, vegetables are juicy, tasty because of the moon rays, sun rays, and it is Jupiter, Mars, Venus, Mercury, Rahu Ketu, all different rays are there, we are always influenced by these rays, the influence of these planets, because of influence of these planets we suffer or we enjoy certain planets are considered to be destructive planets like Saturn it is considered to be a destructive planet.

28.00 mars are considered to be a destructive planet, Rahu Ketu also is a destructive planet, if you see mars means army, police they are all very cruel or very aggressive, fearsome they punish or they destroy things, war comes means aggression, aggressively attacking we have to use our weapon mars is fearsome, aggressive it is considered to be malefic planet destruction happens also mars also protects us from destruction, cruel planet, Saturn, mass destruction, a mass pandemic maybe through some accidents, vehicle accidents.

29.00 Train accidents, air accident or ship accident or an earthquake or tsunami or mass destruction of people it is attributed to Saturn pandemic is attributed to Saturn, Saturn is very strong it is in its own sign Makara Rashi and it will continue to stay in Kumbha Rasi next 2 and half years, next few years will be a challenging period there will be mass destruction, there is also creation, there is destruction again there will be creation Saturn is considered to be a destructive planet, Rahu Ketu they are also considered to be a destructive planet, mercury they are creative planet, there are various book is published, sports are taught, Mercury business.

30.00 Sales purchase, wealth (mercury) Kubera it is a creative planet Venus also creative planet because of Venus there is love, there is marriage, there is childbirth, it is all Venus, and then we have maintenance this world is maintained by administrators, the government is maintaining us, the sun is administrator, he is maintaining us with its heat and light, and we have moon which is maintaining us with its pleasant rays, pleasing rays.

31.00 Because of trees and plants we could able live peacefully otherwise we cannot tolerate the heat of the sun because of the plants we could able to survive In this planet otherwise sun rays is very difficult to survive, we cannot survive in the sun rays, in the present we can survive only on the pleasant atmosphere there are a lot of trees and plants we are nourished by this plants and trees, we get various medicinal herbs, vegetables, we all are nourished by these fruits, medicines it is all coming from moon planet, by the influence of the rays of the moon we are nourished.

32.00 moon planet is pleasing to everyone demons like darkness, they want enjoyment sense enjoyment they like the moon planet more, sun planet makes us work hard, sun planet is full of light demons do not like light they always want to stay in darkness, so we are all controlled by these different planets, there is a creative planet, there is a planet which maintains there is a planet which destroys, administrators are maintaining us, ksatriya planets, brahmana planets are Venus, Jupiter they are giving us knowledge, arts, dance, music, marriage life, this is all Venus and then Jupiter.

33.00 It is a divine planet, Temple worship Scriptural Knowledge, application of Scriptural Knowledge, festivals all these comes under Jupiter and we also have mars, army or commander in chief of demigods, mars, sun, moon administrative planets, Moon is queen, Sun is king, and then we have. Mercury is prince, Jupiter is a minister, Venus is a minister Saturn is considered to be Servant. 7 planets are there Rah kethu are considered to be shadow planets solar or lunar eclipses occurs because of Rahu and Ketu Especially Rahu, Rahu Covers sun and moon for a period of one muhurta or 48 minutes Because of which we experience solar or lunar eclipses it is considered to be inauspicious event, but ultimately we have to take positive aspects the negative aspects there is a destruction of the bad element, we have to consider various bad qualities in us god is destroying all the bad qualities in us, so we fight among ourselves and our bad qualities are destroyed by fighting amongst ourselves, in the past lord was killing the evil spirits, now we are fighting amongst ourselves and getting destroyed ourselves, in the past lord was killing the evil spirits, now we are fighting ourselves getting destroyed ourselves.

35.00 So our Bad qualities are destroyed when there is a lunar or solar eclipse we considered destruction of bad elements/Qualities, good people will not be destroyed, bad people only will be destroyed. Some destruction will happen, some people take to monkhood, many people renounce the material enjoyment they take to spiritual life we have to consider this time is suitable for spiritual progress, spiritual austerity, favorable for austerities, so we have to utilize this opportunity for engaging in austerity chant more hare Krishna maha-mantra, we have to read Srimad Bhagavatam, Bhagavad Gita

36.00 Take advantage of all this time, we have to spend more time with family members, read more Prabhupada's books, cook for the lord, offer bhoga for the lord and offer to your ancestors offer to Vaishnavas, offer to ancestors, children's, family members, offer to neighbors, offer to animals, bird, also try to satisfy all, that is the householder life they are like parents, they have to take care of sanyasis, take care of brahmacharis, also it is the responsibility householders to take care of other family members

37.00 Brahmacharis, grihasthas, vanaprasthas, sanyasis they are dependent on grihastha, so please donate for sanyasis brahmacharis at an ISKCON Temple nearby you, they are suffering because of this pandemic so whatever money you have whatever talent you have always engage it in Krishna's service because Krishna is the enjoyer of all the austerities, sacrifices we perform, he is the master of universe he is the friend of all living entities, he gives everything for us, whatever we want the earth, water, ether, air, fire, mind, intelligence, false ego everything is given to us by lord Krishna so we have to engage everything in the service of Lord Krishna that is the right utilization.

38.00 We are all blessed by Krishna, blessed by Radharani then we will be happy in our life so we should not take the property of god and utilize it in our sense gratification we have to utilize it in Krishna's service, then Krishna also reciprocated, ye yatamam prapadyante tams tathaiva bhajamyaham, we serve Krishna he reciprocates, So I request all of you to donate to Vaishnavas, ISKCON Devotees donate to nearby ISKCON Devotees. I request all of you to serve Vaishnavas we need the blessings of all to lead a happy life. Not to hurt anybody.

39.00 So let's pray together to Krishna such that this pandemic will soon end, let's pray together, let's chant together, let's read Bhagavad Gita together, let this pandemic end as soon as possible, Thank you very much hare Krishna

Hare Krishna Hare Krishna Krishna Krishna Hare Hare

Hare Rama Hare Rama Rama Rama Hare Hare

If you have any doubts, questions please contact me and I will be able to reply to that my mobile number is 9611243737 please contact this number I will try to answer your questions, also I request you to donate to us as much as possible to further improve our preaching activities, online preaching projects, we are using various software's, we want to use professional versions of that software's, pay for some water, electricity, bills, food expenses, struggling with the pandemic, I request all of you to donate us in this tough situations, every one of us is in a difficult situation, as much as possible please donate We don't mind even if it is a small amount, Jay Srila Prabhupada.

CHAPTER SEVEN

Future Predictions

What will happen in Kaliyuga is already being foretold in Srimad Bhagavatha puranam 5100 years ago, people in kali yuga will be lazy, misguided, unfortunate, day by day dharma, truthfulness, cleanliness, forgiveness, mercifulness, longevity, strength, memory will decline, people will be interested in irreligious things like meat-eating, gambling, intoxication, illicit sex.

They are worshipping and glorifying false heroes ex: cinema stars, false gods ex: so many so-called babas, so-called Paramahamsa, so-called Bhagavan's claiming themselves as a god, etc false gurus ex: APA sampradayas or who don't come under proper guru shishya parampara.

Krishnastu Bhagavan swayam Krishna is the supreme god, Ruler he takes various incarnations like, Rama who killed rakshasa Ravana, and ruled the earth as the emperor, Krishna killed various asuras, rakshasas and protected the citizens, Parashurama killed all the evil kings who harm, snatch the property of innocent citizens, Varaha killed hiranyaksa, Narasimha killed hiranyakasipu.

His devotees like Arjuna, Bhima, Yudhisthira, and Pariksit are true warriors and rulers who fought against the evil forces protecting the lives, property of people and established peace and prosperity in the world.

CHAPTER EIGHT

Nivar Cyclone

Speaker

Ramananda Caitanya Candra Das

0:01 Hare Krishna today it's very heavily, continuously raining here (in my village) due to Cyclone, nivara cyclone, there is a continuous rain here, heavy rain, constant rain. So, this life is unsteady. Sometimes there is happiness sometimes there is distress this material world is full of distress, dukhalayam asasvatam, lord Krishna himself has said in bhagavad Gita, dukhalayam asasvatam, whereas Krishna's planet is full of happiness, unending happiness, and eternality, full of knowledge. Now we are in the material world, this is Krishna's creation this is his lower creation, Krishna's higher creation is in the spiritual world. Krishna's lower energy is this material world; we are called lord Krishna's marginal energy. There are living entities who are eternally liberated there are living entities who are eternally conditioned. There are living entities who get liberated by sadhana or bhakti. So, krpa siddha by Mercy, by mercy of Lord Krishna many people become liberated by sadhana by austerity some people become liberated. So sadhana Siddha kripa siddha. So, there are various ways of attaining perfection, one is through austerities. Another is through mercy.

2.00

Just like you have exam you study well, write exam, get the distinction, get high marks, and pass out. That's one point. Another point is somehow grace marks are being allotted to you, just pushing on you so that we vacate the place. Grace marks mercy Like That Lord Krishna is showing mercy in kaliyuga. He has taken the form of a devotee, mood of a woman; mood of Radharani has become caitanya Mahaprabhu. He has a male form, but the mood of Radharani mood of devotee mood of Radharani. So he is very much submissive, loving he is distributing the love of God to all.

3.00.

Irrespective of qualification. Namo Maha vadanyaya Krishna prema pradayate Krishnaya, Krishna caitanya namne goura tvise namaha. This is a mantra by rupa gosvami. So Lord Krishna as Caitanya mahaprabhu is considered to be magnanimous incarnation of all incarnations. Caitanya mahaprabhu is the most munificent incarnation, most charitable incarnation of all the incarnations of Lord Krishna. That's why he is called Maha vadanyaya avatara. So he is Krishna himself. And he is giving Krishna prema to all of us. Only one who has love of God can give us the love of God.

4.00. Sri Caitanya Mahaprabhu is giving us the love of God. He has taken the mood of Radharani, Radha Krishna Nahe Anya Radha and Krishna, there is no difference. So Caitanya Mahaprabhu most merciful incarnation has appeared in kaliyuga, 400 years back, and he has inaugurated the sankirtana movement. That same sankirtana movement is spreading throughout the world. It's because of the efforts of the many acharyas sad goswamis, Jiva Goswami., Bhaktivinoda Thakur. Bakthisiddanta sarasvathi thakur, bhaktivedanta swami Srila prabhupad and many of his disciples, prominent disciples.

5.00

So they all are doing, great services to Lord Krishna to Srila prabhupad. So many disciples of Srila prabhupad have established many temples, having got the training under Srila prabhupada. They have established many centers, many ISKCON centers, temples, that's flourishing nicely all over the world. So it's our duty to take advantage of this harinam sankirtan movement. So we have to chant Hare Krishna mantra, read Srila Prabhupada books distribute Srila prabhupada books. Take Krishna prasadam, Thank you

Hare Krishna Hare Krishna Krishna Krishna Hare Hare Hare Rama
Hare Rama Rama Rama Hare Hare.

6.00

So we are so much proud of our technological advancement. But in front of God, nothing can stand. Just see this thunderstorm and heavy rain, Cyclone. All our mobile towers are stopped working or it's not working. I'm not getting tower now. There is a heavy rain, continuous rain. There's a cyclone. There's a heavy wind. Absolute darkness here. Power has gone. Power is not their here, absolute darkness. Continuously raining. Heavy wind, absolute darkness everywhere. There is no power, mobile tower is not working. Such is the situation in which I'm staying now. This is how this world is there.

7.00 We are proud of our material advancement; we are proud of our technological advancement whatever maybe the advancement. We have placed our satellites ISRO, NASA so many satellites we have placed but no use for us now. There is no power there is no mobile tower. Network is not coming, there is no power here absolute darkness. No communication. So what will we do we are too much dependent on this communication system. Mobile, internet, android phone or whatever it may be, we are proud of all this advancement. But in front of the nature in front of demigods power, God's power nothing can stand

8.00

Absolutely no power, I'm not able to connect to the network. It is saying not registered on network. Due to this rain, this wind and here there is no power also absolute darkness here. Constantly raining everywhere it is water and everywhere it is moisture, heavy wind, freezing cold, absolute darkness what a Hellish situation this is if you want to say hellish situation this is hellish situation. We are experiencing hell sometimes in this earth also.

9.00

So creation, Maintenance destruction is always happening. So destruction maybe because of excessive rain or because of no rain. Maybe because of floods. Volcanoes, Cyclone, earthquake. Whatever it may be ativrsti, anavrsti excessive rain or no rain, excessive wind, excessive coldness, excessive heat. Rainy season, summer, winter everywhere it is still happening. We are always troubled by these three fold miseries that are miseries through body, mind, miseries through other living entities, miseries through natural calamities like nivar cyclone, natural calamities.

10.00.

We are always troubled by these three fold miseries in this world they are adhyatmika, adhiboutika, adhideivika, these are the three fold miseries, and Cyclone is adhideivika. Very powerful. You cannot do anything with divine power, demigod's power. You cannot do anything with this. Certain things we can try to rectify or remedy, but these divine powers, demigods power we cannot do anything. This is constantly happening.

CHAPTER NINE

Live Life Anxiety Free

LIVE LIFE ANXIETY FREE

Sri-prahlada uvaca

tat sadhu manye 'sura-varya dehinam

sada samudvigna-dhiyam asad-grahat

hitvatma-patam grham andha-kupam

vanam gato yad dharim asrayeta

Translation

Prahlada Maharaja replied: O best of the asuras, King of the demons, as far as I have learned from my spiritual master, any person who has accepted a temporary body and temporary household life is certainly embarrassed by anxiety because of having fallen in a dark well where there is no water but only suffering. One should give up this position and go to the forest [vana]. More clearly, one should go to Vrndavana, where only Krishna consciousness is prevalent, and should thus take shelter of the Supreme Personality of Godhead.

Purport

Hiranyakasipu thought that Prahlada, being nothing but a small boy with no actual experience, might reply with something pleasing but nothing practical. Prahlada Maharaja, however, being an exalted devotee, had acquired all the qualities of education.

yasyasti bhaktir bhagavaty akincana

sarvair gunais tatra samasate surah

harav abhaktasya kuto mahad-guna

manorathenasati dhavato bahih

"One who has unflinching devotional faith in Krishna consistently manifests all the good qualities of Krishna and the demigods. However, he who has no devotion to the Supreme Personality of Godhead has no good qualifications because he is engaged by mental concoction in material existence, which is the external feature of the Lord." (Bhag. 5.18.12) So-called educated philosophers and scientists who are simply on the mental platform cannot distinguish between what is actually sat, eternal, and what is asat, temporary. The Vedic injunction is asato mā jyotir gama: everyone should give up the platform of temporary existence and approach the eternal platform. The soul is eternal, and topics concerning the eternal soul are actually knowledge. Elsewhere it is said, apasyatām atma-tattvan gṛhesu grha-medhinam: those who are attached to the bodily conception of life and who thus stick to life as a grhastha, or householder, on the platform of material sense enjoyment, cannot see the welfare of the eternal soul. Prahlada Maharaja confirmed this by saying that if one wants success in life, he should immediately understand from the right sources what his self-interest is and how he should mold his life in spiritual consciousness. One should understand himself to be part and parcel of Krishna and thus completely take shelter of His lotus feet for guaranteed spiritual success. Everyone in the material world is in the bodily conception, struggling hard for existence, life afterlife. Prahlada Maharaja, therefore, recommended that to stop this material condition of repeated birth and death, one should go to the forest (vana).

In the varnasrama system, one first becomes a brahmacari, then a gṛhastha, a vanaprastha and finally a sannyasi. Going to the forest means accepting vanaprastha life, which is between grhastha life and sannyasa. As confirmed in the Visnu Purana (3.8.9), varnsramacaravata purusena parah puman visnur aradhyate: by accepting the institution of varna and asrama, one can very easily elevate himself to the platform of worshiping Visnu, the Supreme Personality of Godhead. Otherwise, if one remains in the bodily conception, one must rot within this material world, and his life will be a failure. Society must have divisions of brahmaṇa, ksatriya, vaisya, and sudra, and for spiritual advancement, one must gradually develop as a brahmacari, gṛhastha, vanaprastha, and sannyasi. Prahlada Maharaja recommended that his father accept vanaprastha life because as a gṛhastha he was becoming increasingly demoniac due to bodily attachment. Prahlāda recommended to his father that accepting vanaprastha life would be better than going deeper and deeper into gṛham andha-kupam, the blind well of life as a grhastha. In our Krishna consciousness movement we, therefore, invite all the elderly persons of the world to come to Vrndavana and stay there in retired life, making advancement in spiritual consciousness, Krishna consciousness.

Speaker : Ramananda Caitanya Candra das

This sloka is very important, informative, and decisive. This is a conversation between Prahlada maharaja and his father hiranyakashipu they belong to daitya or asura family, inimical towards lord Krishna or they are enemies of demigods and Lord Vishnu. Even though he has taken his birth in a daitya family. He is a great devotee he is a mahajana so he become devotee by the teachings of Narada muni, when he was in the womb of his mother Narada muni advised his mother, so in that way, he got to know about devotional services

8.00 from Narada muni within the womb of his mother, he learned to perform devotional service to Lord Krishna when he was still an unborn baby, so here he is explaining to his father they both are discussing in a friendly way, he is addressing his father oh best among the asuras king of demons as far as I have learned from my spiritual master Narada muni, any person who has accepted the temporary body, temporary household life is certainly embarrassed by anxiety because of having fallen in the dark well where there is no water but only suffering so this temporary householder life, temporary body

9.00 asuras are too much attached to the body. Temporary household life, certainly have anxiety as to how to maintain this body, maintain the house how to maintain relatives, friends, so many things, how to give charity, because of acceptance of temporary body they will be in anxiety, when we do it as Krishna's service it becomes a source of our joy but when we do it as a sense gratification that will be the cause for all types of anxiety, so the body, household life is temporary. If we engage everything in Krishna's service then there will be no more anxiety, it will be a source of joy or happiness, but if we do not engage the body in Lord Krishna's service that will be the source of all types of anxiety. Relatives will be like plunderers when we do not possess wealth they will not care for us when we have accumulated lot's of wealth by hard labor everyone will be behind us to plunder the hard-earned wealth, so like this, It will happen, family members like brothers/sisters, children, wife, parents, are like plunderers, when you do not have they will not have time to think about you whereas when you have money they will be behind you to snatch it from you, please give this, give that. So you cannot come out of this dark well so on account of this we will be always in anxiety.

This is the meaning of this verse where there is no happiness but only suffering. We are always thinking that this problem is going to be solved today but immediately another problem will come; it is like a dark well where there is no water but only suffering so it is like a desert. You may be getting a little bit of happiness. In family life, it is compared to a drop of water in a desert. We will not be able to overcome this difficult life.

11.00 Because there is nobody to rescue you from this difficult situation. Only by surrendering to Krishna, we will be able to overcome this difficult situation, if we remain as a grahamedhis envious householders it is extremely difficult, this is an instruction to envious householders or grahamedhis. Grahasthas have surrendered everything to lord Krishna marobi rakhobi jo iccha tomara arpilu tuvapada nandakishora my house, relatives, wealth, everything is surrendered unto you, either you protect me or kill me I surrender everything to you this is the mood of Srila Bhaktivinoda Thakur an ideal family man. Grahamedhis are too much attached to this body and household life

12.00 it is better to give up such a house and go to the forest and do penance, especially holy places like Vrindavana, in holy places it is easier to remember lord Vishnu and to practice devotional services, there are many holy places all over India like Mayapur, Jagannath Puri, Vrindavan, Dwarka, Srirangam, Tirupathi, Kanchipuram, So many holy places are there all over India at the time of old age one has to retire and engage in devotional service to Lord Krishna.

So hiranykashipu thought that Prahlada being a small boy will speak something pleasing nothing practical, Prahlada maharaja however being an exalted devotee had acquired all the good qualities by his devotion

13.00

"Yasyasti bhakthi bhagavathi akinchana sarvaih tatra samasate surah harav abhakthasya kutoh mahad gunah Manorathena asato davatah bahih"

One who has unflinching faith in devotional service to Lord Krishna can consistently manifest all the good qualities of Lord Krishna and demigods. However, he who has no devotion to the Supreme Personality of Godhead has no good qualities, because he is engaged in the mental concoction, material existence which is the external feature of the lord, so there may be many very good material qualifications among people who are non-devotees. But it is just a mental concoction.

But if one is a devotee of Lord Krishna even though he may not be having many good qualities still he is better situated than nondevotee

14. Because he will develop all the desirable good qualities slowly by being in the association of lord Krishna and his dear devotees. Good

qualities will keep on changing among non-devotees. But the good qualities will be consistently manifest in a pure devotee of Lord Krishna Vishnu bhakta bhaved devah asuras tad viparyayah Lord Vishnu bhaktas will have many good qualities, asuras may have good qualities but it will be according to his needs. Their main disqualification is that they are nondevotees and are inimical towards Lord Vishnu.

There are so many well-educated philosophers, scientists they are hovering simply on the mental platform they cannot distinguish between what is sat —real what is asat-unreal, Vedic injunction is asatoma sad gamah tamasomah jyotirgamah" everyone should give up the platform of temporary existence and approach eternal platform this world is full of darkness so it is recommended to go to light called brahmjyoti.

15.00 All the spiritual planets are situated in brahmajyoti just like in the material world all the planets are situated in sunshine similarly in the spiritual world all the planets are situated in Brahma Jyoti effulgence coming from the body of Lord Vishnu. So we all have to go from temporary world to eternal Spiritual world, Soul is eternal there are eight material elements Earth, water, ether, air, fire, mind, intelligence false ego. People have to learn to study the nature of the soul which is very important all above said material elements will keep changing its state of existence but the soul will always remain unchanged s

16.00 apasyatamatma tattvam grihesu grihamedhinam

So grihamedhis will be too much attached to the body, family, house, place of birth, Country, What happens when they don't give up the household life and they don't take up spiritual life is they likely to take birth in the same village, or family or country or they may even become some durdevata or ghost in this way cycle continues those who are attached to bodily conception of life and are a householder on the platform of material sense enjoyment or they will repeatedly take birth and die.

17.00 Human form of life is an opportunity to understand the eternal nature of the soul and engage oneself in that eternal platform. But grihamedhis are attached to the temporary body on account of ignorance of their Eternal self they are engaged in bodily activities for them there is no permanent happiness they will repeatedly take birth and die. So we all have to follow the guru parampara

18.00 Otherwise some people will mislead us like there are so many governmental authorities or politicians, film, sports stars, So many so-called babas, Swamis, Misleading human society to enjoy this temporary body, which is a wrong platform, We have to approach the guru parampara, Ramanujacharya, Madhvacharya, Nimbarka, Vishnu Swami, Like that so many acharyas are there, We have to follow in the footsteps of acharyas then only we will able to understand the reality of this world otherwise people will mislead and exploit us all the above-mentioned men will not inform us to surrender unto Lord Krishna or reveal that we are part and parcel of Lord Krishna.

19.00 They will simply exploit and cheat us they will keep us always in ignorance. So in the city life, it is very difficult to follow Spiritual life So much distraction will be there like T.V. Cinema, Mobile, Internet, So much illusion is there it is not easy to practice spiritual life in the congested cities, Better to go to some solitary places like a resort, village, holy places and practice our Devotional services.

20.00 Otherwise it is extremely difficult, if an ISKCON Centre is nearby it is good otherwise we should try to develop one center or we can go to the places where there are devotees.

In the varnashrama System one first becomes a brahmachari, then grihastha, then vanaprastha, and at last takes up sannyasa ashrama so in this way gradual progress is happening, From boyhood to youth

Author Intro

Author intro

Born in Tamil Nadu, Did Schooling, Completed college Education in Bangalore, Introduced to Krishna consciousness in the year 2003, got initiated into Gaudiya Vaishnavism in the year 2019 by His Holiness Jayapataka Swami Maharaj, initiated name Ramananda Caitanya Candra das, Attended various seminars, Lectures on Srimad Bhagavatham, Bhagavad Gita, full time, Did various volunteer services to ISKCON Society at Bangalore, Vrindavan, Have completed graduation from Agra University, Visited various temples in India, Visited various pilgrimage centers in India, Savaman Saligram Temple, Loi Bazaar, Did Parikrama of Vrindavan, visited various holy places in Vrindavan Brij Mandal.

Author Introduction

Hare Krishna, this is Ramananda Caitanya Chandra das, I'm the author of books The Secret to Success, Brahma Jnana and Tantra Jnan, Time, and Rule of Saintly Kings, I'm also working on many small books for the sake of preaching. Basically, I preach online I use platforms like YouTube, and social networking websites, I also preach in villages of R.K.Pettai, Pallipattu, Tiruttani Tulukas of Tiruvallur District, sometimes I travel to other places, other centers. I assist them in their Preaching activities. I also help in resolving many managerial issues in ISKCON Centres. Sometimes I go on pilgrimage tours, I have resided at many holy places like Mathura, Vrindavan, Ahobilam, Mayapur, Jagannath Puri. In some places, I just visited whereas in places like Vrindavan I have stayed for quite a long time. As for as my schooling and college education is concerned it was in Bangalore. whereas my graduation was by distance education through Dr.B.R.Ambedkar University, Agra during this time I was residing at Vrindavan, Mathura district of Uttar Pradesh.

Education is a continuous process so I learn every day, even today I learn something new, So learning is a lifetime process, it is not that I learned everything, so we always keep learning every day. So, since 2003 I'm connected with ISKCON society. And I have seen various things in ISKCON, I have done various services for ISKCON. like book distribution, prasadam distribution Selling of Puja, Archana tickets, Coconut sales. Coconut breaking services, Queue management, and Youth preaching, Book distribution in trains and in buses, in the streets, and during Krishna

Janmashtami festivals assisting in pot cleaning, abishekam, assistant pujari services, Cooking assistant, guest hospitality, harinama sankirtan, and meditation classes. in this way, many services are rendered by me.

I have participated or assisted in many Similar programs. Also, I have traveled to many places in India like Mangalore, Dharmasthala Kukke Subramanya, Mysuru, Nanjangudu, Tumkur, Kolar, Shimoga, I Have participated in Vishva gou sammelana organized by Ramachandra pura mutt, Hosanagara, Shimoga District of Karnataka, We have distributed Srila Prabhupada books in that event. On many occasions, I have distributed books on running trains at the following routes Jolarpettai, Hassan, Mysuru, etc

6.00 I have also rendered services at ISKCON Mangalore, for about three months during these periods I have visited Udupi Krishna temple several times, I have also participated in various Ratha yatras conducted in Bangalore, Mysuru, Mangalore, Chennai, Puri, etc I have visited many holy places India like Mathura, Vrindavan, Ahobilam, Mayapur, Jagannath Puri, Hyderabad, yadagirigutta, Srirangam, Tirunelveli, Kanyakumari, Tirupathi I used to visit on a regular basis, I have visited many temples in cannanore, kumbal godu, at Kerala state

7.00 I had interaction with various Srila Prabhupada disciples, I was a regular visitor of ISKCON Krishna Balaram Mandir, in Vrindavan, In this temple, Srila Prabhupada Samadhi mandir has been built by the devotees, I used to sit here and chant hare Krishna maha-mantra, I used to regularly visit many important temples of Vrindavan, Mathura, Govardhan in the entire Braja Mandal area.

8.00 We had a very close connection with Radha Shyam Sundar, Radhagopinath, Radhadamodar Temple Goswami's, In the Radharaman temple I used to sit and chant the hare Krishna maha-mantra. Radha Shyam Sundar, Radhagopinath, Radhadamodar, Radharaman, Radhamadan Mohan, Radhavinod, Radhagovinda, Vrindavan Parikrama, Yamuna Arati, and Yamuna Darshan, I had interaction with various Srila Prabhupada disciples, Many Russian, Australian, Malaysian, Srilankan, Bangladeshi, Switzerland, Croatia, Canada and foreign devotees.

9.00 Russian pujari was rendering service to Srila Prabhupada bhajan kutir at Radhadamodar temple, I used sit chant hare Krishna maha-mantra, that devotee used to offer me some prasadam from the plate of Srila Prabhupada, I used to live along with Krishna kishore Prabhu Who was the former pujari at Srila Prabhupada bhajan kutir in Radhadamodar temple,

Birthday Message 2020
Hare Krishna Hare Krishna Krishna Krishna Hare Hare
Hare Rama Hare Rama Rama Rama Hare Hare
01
Hare Krishna Today 03.09.2020. Historical day for me 35 years back I was born on this same day In a small village outside of Chennai city, Gummidipoondi, 36th birthday this is a very important day for me, on this important day, I just wanted to share some of my experiences with ISKCON Movement, Srila Prabhupada in the year 2003 I got introduced to Krishna consciousness since then I have started practicing Krishna consciousness.

2.00

My college is was there Vivekananda College, Rajajinagar, and Bangalore
Just Opposite to that is ISKCON temple

I got an invitation for Youth programs, I accepted the invitation and have attended the programs Weekend Yoga Retreat Programmes

Library also

2.24

And like that got introduced to Krishna consciousness through youth programs, Like Friends of Lord Krishna, Srila Prabhupada's books, I used to listen Prabhupada lectures, I used to go to temples, Associate with devotees, chant Hare Krishna Maha Mantra and then attend temple programmes, Festivals also

3.00 Krishna Janmastami, Gour Poornima I used to do lot of services, Book Distribution, Prasadam cooking distribution, Abhiskeam Pot cleaning, Mandira Marjana Seva, Queue management, Chappal stand, Coconut Breaking, Pushpanjali Seva, Archana Seva, like that many services I used to do, Pancajanya vehicle, for book distribution locations like Mysore,

4.30.

Indranagar, Jayanagar, banshakari, in trains, Routes like Jolarpettai, Hassan, Mysore also many many locations in trains, in bus, also in temple like that many things.

5.00

www.ingramcontent.com/pod-product-compliance
Lightning Source LLC
Chambersburg PA
CBHW050618160726
48003CB00003B/1242